Nottingham
Inns and

on old picture postcards

**Designed and Published by
Reflections of a Bygone Age,
Keyworth, Nottingham
1990**

Victoria Station & Hotel, Nottingham.

Victoria Hotel – Nottingham. The Victoria Hotel with its 167 bedrooms was built at the same time as the adjacent Victoria Station, and received its licence in 1901. It has survived much better than the station, which, apart from the tower only lasted 67 years. 'Clumber' series card no. 351, published by A. Hindley.

Valentine's of Dundee published this card of "The Gate Hangs Well" on Castlegate. It was postally used from Derby in August 1908, when Nathan S. Woodward was licensee.

The Bell Inn – Angel Row, Nottingham. The Bell, situated close to the bustling Market Place, can just be seen as the third building up on the left of this postcard, published by William Ritchie & Sons of Edinburgh, and posted from Nottingham in April 1908. The oldest parts of the building are the cellars, reputed to be from Anglo-Saxon times. Originally there were monastic buildings on the site. Since the turn of the century it has been in the hands of the Jackson family. The writer of the card, Arthur Teale, wrote to his friend in Newport: *"This is, I suppose, the centre of Nottingham, though of course it is very flattering. Near is the market, which is simply a collection of booths which are pulled down afterwards."*

**Printed by
Adlard Print and Typesetting Services,
Ruddington, Notts.**

ISBN 0 946245 31 2

£2.95

INTRODUCTION

A study of the Pubs and Inns of Nottinghamshire provides a fascinating insight into life in the past reflecting the changing needs and fashions of society. Inns had a variety of roles to play ranging from providing food and lodging to weary travellers, to serving as social centres and meeting places for the local populace.

The drinking of ale has been a way of life for centuries, and even the smallest village had at least one inn. In 1901, for instance, there were recorded 574 pubs in Nottingham alone.

As needs have changed, so have the places themselves. Many buildings have been lost to road widening (The Sherwin Arms, Bramcote) or improved housing needs (Oliver Cromwell Inn – St. Anns) whilst others like the Black Boy in Nottingham have been judged surplus to requirements and demolished.

Demographic changes have made some pubs redundant and often these have reverted to private houses (The Unicorn at Bulcote).

Changing fashions have accounted for alterations to some pub buildings (Saracen's Head – Southwell) or even to their names (The Neville Arms – Kinoulton) and the three temperance inns in the book are now all fully licensed.

It is hoped that this book will give as much pleasure as the pubs and inns on the postcards have given to their customers over the years.

Picture Postcards were first published in Britain in 1894, but it was not until a decade later that they began to take off, when in 1902 the Post Office allowed a message to be written on the address side. This meant that the whole of one side was available for the picture and obviously gave more scope to publishers. Photographic viewcards became very popular, and the postcard became the most important way of communicating news or messages, in much the same way as the telephone is used today. The years up to 1914 were the 'Golden Age' of picture postcards, when millions of imaginative designs covering every subject under the sun were published by a host of national and local firms. There's hardly a village or hamlet that wasn't documented at that time by a postcard publisher, though sometimes the number of cards available was unrelated to the size of a community.

The postcards in this book are the work of a variety of publishers, ranging from local ones like Spree or Albert Hindley's 'Clumber' series to big national firms like Valentine of Dundee, Wrench of London, or Frith of Reigate. Sometimes the cards have an added bonus in the form of a message or interesting postmark on the reverse. Nowadays, they're keenly sought by collectors as images of a vanished past or evidence of changing scenes.

Dave Ottewell, October 1990

1. The Flying Horse – Nottingham. Sadly The Flying Horse has recently been allowed to close as an inn, and is now a shopping arcade. Its buildings date from Elizabethan times, and at one stage it was known as 'The Travellers'. It consists of a group of smaller buildings joined together. The façade has undergone various stages of beautification. This postcard is no. **5291** in the 'Pelham' Real Photo Series, published by Boots.

2. The Salutation Inn – Nottingham. Most of the inn's building dates from the 15th century with some of its rock-hewn cellars thought to date from even earlier. Being so close to the castle, it has witnessed many historical events, including acting as a recruiting office for the Royalist cause in the Civil War. 'Rex' series postcard no. 170.

3. The Trip to Jerusalem Inn – Nottingham. This major tourist attraction claims to be the oldest inn in England, dating from 1189 and at one time the brewhouse for the Castle. It is said that crusaders stopped here on the way to the Holy Lands, hence its name. Some of the inn's rooms go back into the rocks on which Nottingham Castle is situated. Many claim the inn is not as old as it is reputed to be, but it is still a fascinating place to visit. 'Rex' series card no. 141.

4. Oliver Cromwell Inn – St. Anns, Nottingham. There were many large pubs and inns in the Nottingham suburbs at the turn of the century. In 1905 the Oliver Cromwell's publican was Thomas Edwin Booth, selling Hawkins Ales. Redevelopment work eventually saw the end of this popular inn. The postcard, by W.H. Smith & Son, was published about 1910, and also features a no. 62 tram and Crouch's delivery wagon in Commercial Square.

5. The Mansfield Arms – Nottingham. A superb photographic card showing the pub around 1920, when the licensee was George W. Medcalf. A crowd has been specially assembled for the photograph, which also features the Victoria station frontage and clocktower. It's now called 'Ledgers'.

6. The Talbot – Long Row, Nottingham. The Talbot can be seen to the left of this Clumber Series (no. 127) postcard. It was built in 1876, on the site of a much older inn, by Edward Barker Cox, a wealthy local steel bar manufacturer. It was once described as the *"biggest gin palace in the Midlands".* It was an aladdins cave inside, full of paintings and statues.

7. Black Boy Hotel – Long Row, Nottingham. To many people, myself included, the city planners of Nottingham have made many mistakes in the pursuit of so-called progress. The demolition of this beautiful building, to be replaced by an ugly shop front, is one of the worst examples. There had been an hotel on this site for many years and in 1887 the illustrious Nottingham architect, Watson Fothergill, had designed the building on the postcard, sadly now only a fond memory.

8. Sir Charles Napier – Nottingham. Superb advertising card for this pub on Sherwood Street, near the Arboretum gates, where it still stands.

9. Lord Nelson Inn – Sneinton, Nottingham. As this 'Rex' series card (no. 297) shows, this inn began life as a pair of cottages which were knocked into one when conversion to a public house took place about 200 years ago. The cottages are thought to date back a further 300 years, whilst the cellars are caves hollowed out of the sandstone. At one stage it was a coaching inn known as 'Hornbuckles'.

Trent Bridge Inn (Old), Nottingham.

10. Trent Bridge Inn – West Bridgford. This photo dates from before 1885 for it was then that the modern Trent Bridge Inn was built at a cost of £1,600. This older picture is included because of the history associated with the building. It was here in 1838 that the licencee, William Clarke, laid out a cricket ground in a meadow at the rear of the pub which was to become the home of Nottinghamshire cricket and a Test Match ground.

Griffen's Head. Aslockton.

11. Griffin's Head – Whatton. The caption on this card is a puzzle, there being no Griffen's Head in Aslockton. In fact it is The Griffin's Head in the nearby village of Whatton. At the start of the 1930's when this card was sent, William Swingler was the publican. Sadly the buildings have been demolished and there is a new Griffin's Head, a Home Ales pub, on the site. Postcard published by Spree.

MANVERS ARMS & MANOR HOUSE, RADCLIFFE.

12. Manvers Arms – Radcliffe-on-Trent. This Clumber series (no. 17a) card, postally used in 1907, shows a view of The Manvers Arms at Radcliffe-on-Trent. The Manvers family seat was at Thoresby Hall near Ollerton, but the explanation for the Arms being used so far away is that when first created Earl Manvers in 1806, the gentleman already held the title 'Baron Pierrepont', from the village of Holme Pierrepont, near Radcliffe. There is also a pub of the same name at Cotgrave.

13. Cuckoo Bush Inn – Gotham. This building was erected in 1858 on the site of a previous inn of the same name. It takes its name from an act by the "wise men" of Gotham, who in order to keep King John away from the area, decided to act as simpletons. One of their ploys was to build a hedge round a tree in which a cuckoo was perched. When asked why they had done this they said it was to stop the cuckoo flying away! Anonymously-published photographic postcard.

14. Red Lion Hotel – Costock. At the turn of the century, Bradley Truman was mine host of this popular hotel. He made it a haven for music hall performers and many famous names such as Harry Lauder, Marie Lloyd and Dan Leno paid visits. This well-animated Clumber series card (no. 377) was sent in 1917 from East Leake to Leicester.

15. Rancliffe Arms – Bunny. The Rancliffe Arms is remembered for its association with Sir Thomas Parkyns of Bunny Hall. He was passionately interested in wrestling, kept two wrestlers in pay himself, and in 1712 began annual wrestling matches which took place in what are now the grounds of the Rancliffe Arms. The card was published by E.H. Hill of the Post Office, Bunny, probably in the 1930's.

The "Plough," Normanton-on-Soar

16. The Plough – Normanton-on-Soar. The village of Normanton-on-Soar, 3 miles north-west of Loughborough, is right to the south of the county. The Plough, situated on the banks of the River Soar, is a Tudoresque building, but if we go by the date on the front it only dates back to 1856. Today it is an Ind Coope house.

EAST END, KINOULTON.

17. The Neville Arms – Kinoulton. In 1936, when this postcard was sent, the pub was known as The Hind Arms as it was in 1941 when the local directory shows Albert H. Avery as the publican. At some stage in the last forty years, the pub was renamed the 'Neville Arms'. Today it is a Kimberley Ales House. W.H. Smith in Melton Mowbray published the card.

18. Wheatsheaf – Cropwell Bishop. This village inn is still painted white today. In days past its patrons arrived by foot or coach and horses. Today it caters for the modern pub-commuter with a car park situated opposite. In 1904 when this card was published (Clumber series no. 236) the publican was William Hanbury. Now it is a Home Ales house.

19. The White Hart – Lenton. The photographer of this Clumber series card (no. 170) persuaded most of the village children to pose for him. This building dates from about 1800, and on the site previously was a farmhouse that had been turned into Lenton Coffee House. By the side of the inn is the site of the debtors prison, known as Old Peveril Gaol.

20. Admiral Rodney – Wollaton. This Wollaton hostelry is appropriately named after Lord Rodney, the famous sailor, who often visited nearby Wollaton Hall. He also gave his name to the reservoir under the Hall which he daily visited, ostensibly to take a bath but more likely to indulge his passion for ale! It is known as the "Admiral's Bath". Home Brewery purchased the building in 1925, the photo being taken at about this time (Rex series no. 1891).

21. Sherwin Arms – Bramcote. The Sherwin Arms is named after John Sherwin, who in 1805 built Bramcote Hills House. This building was demolished in the 1930's in order to widen Derby Road and Trowell Road. A new pub, with the same name, was erected to the rear of this site. Broomhead, of Bramcote's Post Office Stores, published this card.

22. The Broad Oak Inn – Strelley. Up until 1962, the Broad Oak was part of the Strelley Hall Estate and for many years was run by the People's Refreshment House Association, a temperance movement. The building dates from about 1750, and takes its name from an ancient oak in the Hall Park. It was one of the few inns in Nottingham to have a six-day licence.

23. The Woodlark Inn – Lambley. This picture on a card postally used in June 1919 shows how small the Woodlark Inn was. It takes its name from the bird that frequented the area in the past.

24. The Green Dragon – Oxton. This village inn is around two hundred years old and until the 1920's was part of a dairy farm. In Edwardian times it received carriages from far and wide due to enjoying a good reputation for its high class catering facilities. The farm buildings, which were greater in size than the inn itself, were removed to make way for the car park. A 'Clumber' series card, no. 248.

25. The Marquis of Granby – Hoveringham. This inn in the pleasant village of Hoveringham was built in 1832 and named after the Marquis of Granby, who fought in the Napoleonic Wars. He lived at Belvoir Castle and later became the Duke of Rutland. The card, published by the Doncaster Rotophoto Co. in the 1920's was sent from the village to Cambridgeshire in 1940. *"May wants to go to the Goose Fair with Renee tomorrow"*, went the message.

26. The Old Elm Tree Hotel – Hoveringham. This imposing building is The Old Elm Tree Hotel, situated on the banks of the River Trent at Hoveringham. The original part of the building dates back to the early 17th century, but there have been many extensions to increase it to its present size. It was closed in 1988 and there are now plans to convert it into luxury apartments.

27. Waggon and Horses – Bleasby. This building is over 200 years old and has been so named since at least 1824. When Bradley Truman, the famous tenant of the 'Red Lion' at Costock, found that he could not afford to buy the Red Lion he was obliged to move to smaller premises and came to the Waggon and Horses. He never settled and on his death was taken back to Costock for burial. C. & A.G. Lewis of Nottingham published this postcard as no. 978 in their very fine photographic series of the Midlands.

28. Star and Garter – Bleasby. This impressive building is situated on the banks of the River Trent in the rural backwater of Bleasby. Its situation by the river explains its size, for at this point, known as Hazelford, there was a ferry that transported people across the Trent. Another Lewis card, no. 973.

29. Coach and Horses – Thurgarton. Thurgarton has two public houses within a hundred yards of each other on the main Nottingham to Southwell Road. To the right is the Coach and Horses, whilst what some might claim to be the premier pub in the village (and certainly the oldest) the 'Red Lion', with parts dating from the 16th century, can just be seen at the far end of the row of buildings on the left.

Bulcote, near Nottingham.

30. Unicorn Inn – Bulcote. This 'Clumber' series card (no. 104) shows the old Unicorn Inn but even by the time this card was published in 1905, it had reverted to being a private house. Once it had been a flourishing coaching inn with its own barns and stables and doing its own brewing on the premises. Some claim its decline was due to its close proximity to the village church!

31. The Black Horse – Caythorpe. This quaint building, spoilt by the modern sign, dates from the early 18th century. Its claim to fame is that Dick Turpin, the highwayman, is reputed to have stayed here. A small cupboard-like room with exits to two bars and a window is supposed to have been his quick getaway hiding place. Postcard published as an advertising card in the 1970's by landlord Jack Sherwin.

32. Saracen's Head Hotel – Southwell. The Saracen's Head was until the early 18th century known as the 'King's Head'. It was here that King Charles I had his last meal as a free man before surrendering to the Scottish Commissioners at the time of the Civil War. As this pre-1914 postcard by G.W. Wilson shows, the Saracen's Head has undergone much refurbishment and outward change in recent times.

33. The Admiral Rodney Hotel – Southwell. A little walk down the road from the more famous Saracen's Head is to be found The Admiral Rodney Hotel, as seen on this card by local photographer H. Barrett. An old inn, by tradition some of its beams are said to come from the ship "Rodney", whilst one came from the Minster when a new ringing chamber was constructed. An unusual feature is the recently discovered medieval well on the premises.

34. Ram Hotel/Royal Oak – Newark-on-Trent. Two inns for the price of one! The Ram Hotel and The Royal Oak are situated next to each other on Castle Gate opposite the remains of Newark Castle. There has been an inn on the site since the 14th century, but the present 'Ram' dates from the late 18th century. In 1868 the author George Eliot stayed at the Ram. This postcard, in the Wrench series, was posted at Tuxford in June 1907.

35. The Queen's Head – Newark-on-Trent. As can be seen from this 1940's Valentines' series card, The Queen's Head is an early 16th century building, half-timbered in English oak. It stands in the corner of the Market Place, and underwent restoration in 1960.

36. Ossington Coffee Palace – Newark-on-Trent. This imposing building was constructed as a temperance coffee palace by Viscountess Ossington in 1882. Originally it had stables for 40 horses and was a local meeting place, housing a library and bowling alley. This card was published by Francis Frith of Reigate just prior to the First World War.

37. The Old White Hart – Newark-on-Trent. The Old White Hart is claimed to be the most ancient inn in Newark, with its façade dating from the mid-14th century. In the 1830's it was the main halting place for carriers in the town. At the time of this picture (about 1940) it can be seen to be in decline. Luckily in 1978 it was taken over the The Nottingham Building Society who have carried out a most sympathetic restoration.

38. Clinton Arms Hotel – Newark-on-Trent. Clinton is the family name of the Dukes of Newcastle and Earls of Lincoln. There has been an inn on this site since the 14th century, though this building, with its colonnaded frontage, is Georgian. When the poet Byron stayed here at the beginning of the 19th century, it was known as 'The Kingston Arms'. A little later in 1832 it was the headquarters for William Gladstone's parliamentary campaign. Valentine's of Dundee published the card.

39. The Bromley Arms – Fiskerton. The Bromley Arms must have one of the best sites in the county, situated as it is on the banks of the River Trent facing miles of rolling countryside. It took its name from the Smith and Bromley families who for a long time were resident in the Hall at East Stoke, which is just across the river from Fiskerton. For many years the two villages were linked by a ferry. 'Wrench' series postcard no. 15897, posted at Rolleston in August 1908.

40. The Greyhound Inn – Arnold. Nottingham Road, Arnold is the site of The Greyhound Inn. It was built in the 1830's and at the time this 'Clumber' series card (no. 43) was sent, during the First World War, the publican was William Knight, selling ales from the local Home Brewery.

Nuttall Road, Kimberley, Notts.

41. The Stag Inn – Kimberley. Kimberley is well known in local brewing circles having at one time been home to two breweries, Hardys and Hansons which are now one. This helps to explain why, at the turn of the century , there were so many pubs in the village. The Stag was one of them. E. Bostock ws the publican at the time of this postcard in the 'Alton' series, sent from Kimberley in October 1909.

42. The Sun Inn – Eastwood. The Sun Inn, standing by the market place in D.H. Lawrence's birthplace of Eastwood, has a place in history, being the birthplace of the Midland Railway. It was here in 1832 that a group of local coal owners met and decided to build a railway to improve the distribution of their product. 'Rex' series postcard no. 1505.

43. Queen's Head – Watnall. This inn is over 300 years old and has very much a farmhouse feel to it. Older locals still refer to it as 'Joe Haywood's place': he was landlord from the turn of the century until the outbreak of the second world war. He had been batman to Sir Lancelot Rolleston of Watnall Hall, in the Boer War and as a reward for saving his life had been given the tenancy of the inn. Postcard in the 'Peveril' series.

THE HUT, NEWSTEAD, NOTTS.

44. The Hut – Newstead. This building, situated at the gates of Newstead Abbey Park, has had a chequered history. In the early part of the 19th century it was an inn but by 1868 had become the private home of the chaplain to the owner of Newstead Abbey. By the date of this card (Clumber series no. 641), published in 1905, it had reverted to being an inn, albeit a temperance one.

COPYRIGHT L L· ED·5· MOORGREEN. G. C. BRITTAIN & SONS LTD. EASTWOOD SERIES.

45. Horse and Groom – Moorgreen. This popular hostelry set in D.H. Lawrence country was originally a farmhouse on the Greasley Castle estate. Part of the building dates back to the 17th century and at one time what is now a storeroom at the back acted as the local mortuary. Postcard published by G.C. Brittain in the 'Eastwood' series about 1920.

46. The Horse and Groom – Linby. The building on the right is the Horse and Groom in the picturesque village of Linby. The building itself is over 300 years old and for many years, until 1921, ale was brewed on the premises.

47. Forest Folk Hotel – Blidworth. This large building was opened about 25 years before this card was published in 1926. It took its name from the novel by James Prior Kirk. Coloured glass windows depicting scenes from the book were used to decorate the hotel, and in the last few years these have been moved to a more prominent position in the bar.

48. Huntsman Inn – Torworth. This Welchman Brothers (Retford) card shows the Huntsman Inn in Torworth in the north of the county. The card was posted from Mansfield in June 1921 and the inn has changed little in the intervening years, though the cottages at the far end have disappeared and the wooden fence has gone to make way for the car park.

49. George and Dragon Inn – Scrooby. If you went to find the George and Dragon in Scrooby today you would be in for a disappointment. It is now a private residence which has been tastefully converted and extended. When it lost its licence is a little unclear but as late as the second world war, J. Richmond was the publican selling ale from the property. Doncaster Rotophoto Co. card no. 203-9.

Photo Ashley.

50. The White Hart Hotel – Retford. The White Hart is strategically situated, being a corner building facing out onto Retford Market Place. It is an old coaching inn and for many years was in the hands of the same family, the Dennetts. To the right it can be seen that some of the windows have been bricked up, possibly due to the iniquitous window tax of the eighteenth century.

"WHITE HART," ...rton, Notts.

A. PALING,
Proprietor.

51. The White Hart – Ollerton. This building dates from the 1770's, being on the site of an earlier inn which was destroyed by fire. For over a 100 years it was in the ownership of the Collins family, though at the time of this card, 1907, A. Paling was the proprietor. The postcard is a promotional one for the hotel itself.

52. Hop Pole Hotel – Ollerton. The Hop Pole is a large 18th century hostelry. It grew up to serve some of the coaches which, when travelling north, left the Great North Road near Newark and took the more picturesque route through Ollerton to Worksop before rejoining the Great North Road near Doncaster. Card by the Doncaster Rotophoto Co. (no. 97-20).

53. The Sun Inn – North Wheatley. This card dates from 1920 when Horace Wright Shaw was the publican. Then it sold Hewitts' ales and stouts, while today it is a Free House. It has been modernised and extended to the right hand side and the transport it attracts today is a little different to the beautiful bike combination seen in the foreground. Another Doncaster Rotophoto Co. card, no. 223-7.

54. Royal Oak – North Leverton. North Leverton, famous for its still working windmill is home to the Royal Oak public house. This card was dispatched from the village in 1939. The pub remains much the same today and on a recent visit was very much in need of a coat of paint!

55. Markham Moor Inn – nr. Retford. As can be seen from this Edgar Welchman & Son, Retford, card, the Markham Moor Inn caters for a large passing trade. Being within a stone's throw of the Great North Road it has been a favourite stopping point for weary travellers from the days of coach and horses to the present time.

Egmanton.

56. Old Plough – Egmanton. The quiet backwater of Egmanton, close to Tuxford, is still the home of the Old Plough. Pre-1914, when this photo was taken, Mrs. Mary Brown was the publican. Nothing much has changed in the village though someone has covered the mellow old brick frontage with white paint and the cottage to the left of the pub has now gone. The writer of this card noted that he (or she) was pictured on the front!

57. The Sun Inn – Everton. The Sun Inn at Everton, right to the north of the county, has changed little in the 83 years since this card was sent from the village to the Inland Revenue in Lincoln. However, instead of selling ales from the Farmers Brewery Company Ltd. it is now part of the John Smith's chain of pubs.

NORMANTON INN, CLUMBER

58. Normanton Inn – Clumber. This Kingsway series postcard by W.H. Smith shows the Normanton Inn which is situated on the busy A614 adjacent to the gates of Clumber Park. The building is thought to have been converted from an old manor house.

59. The Angel Inn – Blyth. This famous old coaching inn at Blyth has a long history and indeed there is a bill from the inn in existence dating from 1274. The card, published by Frith of Reigate, was sent from nearby Worksop in 1962 but the picture probably dates from a few years earlier.

60. The Old Bell Hotel – Barnby Moor. The Bell is situated on the Great North Road which accounts for its rise to fame as a coaching inn in the early 18th century. At its peak it had stabling for 120 horses. Its decline was due to the advent of the Great Northern Railway; indeed for a period of about 60 years it was closed as an inn and used as two private houses. The introduction of the horseless carriage saw it re-opened for its former use. Postcard by H.E. Peake, Ipswich.

"The Town Arms," Trent Bridge,
Nottingham.

Telephone 1835.

61. The Town Arms – Trent Bridge. Advertising card postally used in April 1915. The photograph must have been taken just after a Forest game. Still a very popular pub, but called The 'Aviary'.

POSTERN GATE, NOTTINGHAM.

62. The Postern Gate – Nottingham. 'Clumber' series card no. 135, posted in Nottingham in October 1906. This pub stood on the corner of Drury Hill, but was demolished in 1911 – the site later became a Post Office and is now a thoroughfare to Broad Marsh Centre.